To our [illegible]
Bro, On your
birthday 1992.
With lots of
love from Barbie,
Bush + Ally Wally
xxx

# A TREASURY OF *Bush* VERSE

*Selected and Introduced by*
G. A. WILKES

An imprint of HarperCollins*Publishers*

*AN ANGUS & ROBERTSON BOOK*
*An imprint of HarperCollinsPublishers*

*First published in Australia in 1991 by*
*CollinsAngus&RobertsonPublishers Pty Limited (ACN 009 913 517)*
*A division of HarperCollinsPublishers (Australia) Pty Limited*
*Unit 4, Eden Park, 31 Waterloo Road, North Ryde*
*NSW 2113, Australia*

*HaperCollinsPublishers (New Zealand) Limited*
*31 View Road, Glenfield, Auckland 10, New Zealand*

*HarperCollinsPublishers Limited*
*77–85 Fulham Palace Road, London W6 8JB, United Kingdom*



*National Library of Australia*
*Cataloguing-in-Publication data:*

*A Treasury of bush verse.*

*Includes Index.*
*ISBN 0 207 17300 1.*

*1. Australian poetry. 2. Folk poetry, Australian.*
*3. Country life — Australia — Poetry.*

*A821.00803294*

*Cover* A Hot Day, *1888 (Detail), David Davies*
*oil on canvas, 60.6 x 91.3 cm*
*Felton Bequest, 1937*
*National Gallery of Victoria*

*Typeset by Adtype Graphics Pty Ltd, North Sydney*
*Printed in Singapore*

*5 4 3 2 1*
*95 94 93 92 91*

# *Contents*

# Foreword

The population of Australia now lives mainly in the cities. We nevertheless still think of Australia as the 'sunburnt country' or 'the wide brown land'; cricketers and footballers refer to the playing-field as 'the paddock'; every now and then 'Waltzing Matilda' is put forward as a possible national anthem. There is a feeling still that the bush is the real Australia.

There are good reasons for this. The bush first showed Australia as having distinctive features which had no counterpart in the other hemisphere. For the first settlers these were animals, birds, trees and features of landscape, which have come into the vocabulary under their Aboriginal names. But soon there were distinctive human figures as well—the bushranger, the swagman, the shearer, the bullocky—and eventually a whole mode of life that had no real parallel anywhere else.

The poems in this collection are a partial record of that life. The tradition begins with the ballads, which survive in a number of versions and have no known author, but register the world of the convict, the overlander, the stockman and 'the wild colonial boy'. This may be the beginning of the anti-authoritarian strain in Australian literature. There are many poetical flourishes in the ballads, despite their 'folk' quality, but the main literary tradition intervenes with such poets as Harpur, Gordon and Kendall, who bring out the romantic features of the Australian scene. This romantic dimension is not lost in the more sardonic world of Lawson and Paterson in the 1890s, although it takes a different form. The drover and the swagman are 'battlers', committed to a life of hardship: but somehow for Lawson and Paterson they are still heroic figures, superior to the environment in which they move.

The Australian bush tradition has acquired the status of a myth, like the frontier in the United States. This is not to its discredit. A myth must have a reality behind it if it is to endure. These poems all have a celebratory quality, grim as they may sometimes be in their subject matter, or occasionally naive and sentimental in their expression. They have all proved their appeal to 'the common reader', whom Dr Johnson saw as making the final judgment.

I suspect that many others besides myself carry in their heads lines of verse first learnt at school. 'There was movement at the station', 'The faithful dog a moment', 'Life is mostly froth and bubble' — I would have encountered these first in the *School Magazine* at primary school. This has been one guide in putting the selection together. It has been a pleasure to revisit these poems and others like them, and to add some more recent poets who show the tradition persisting.

G. A. Wilkes
Sydney, 1991

# My Country

The love of field and coppice,
Of green and shaded lanes,
Of ordered woods and gardens
Is running in your veins;
Strong love of grey-blue distance,
Brown streams and soft, dim skies —
I know but cannot share it,
My love is otherwise.

I love a sunburnt country,
A land of sweeping plains,
Of ragged mountain ranges,
Of droughts and flooding rains.
I love her far horizons,
I love her jewel-sea,
Her beauty and her terror —
The wide brown land for me!

The stark white ring-barked forests,
All tragic to the moon,
The sapphire-misted mountains,
The hot gold hush of noon.
Green tangle of the brushes,
Where lithe lianas coil,
And orchids deck the tree-tops
And ferns the warm dark soil.

Core of my heart, my country!
Her pitiless blue sky,
When sick at heart, around us,

We see the cattle die —
But then the grey clouds gather,
And we can bless again
The drumming of an army,
The steady, soaking rain.

Core of my heart, my country!
Land of the Rainbow Gold,
For flood and fire and famine,
She pays us back threefold;
Over the thirsty paddocks,
Watch, after many days,
The filmy veil of greenness
That thickens as we gaze.

An opal-hearted country,
A wilful, lavish land —
All you who have not loved her,
You will not understand —
Though earth holds many splendours,
Wherever I may die,
I know to what brown country
My homing thoughts will fly.

DOROTHEA MACKELLAR

# Botany Bay

Farewell to old England for ever,
Farewell to my rum culls as well,
Farewell to the well-known Old Bailey,
Where I used for to cut such a swell.

*Chorus:*
Singing, too-ral, li-ooral, li-addity,
Singing, too-ral, li-ooral, li-ay.
Singing, too-ral, li-ooral, li-addity,
Singing, too-ral, li-ooral, li-ay.

There's the captain as is our commander,
There's the bosun and all the ship's crew,
There's the first- and the second-class passengers,
Knows what we poor convicts goes through.

'Tain't leaving old England we care about,
'Tain't cos we misspells wot we knows,
But because all we light-fingered gentry
Hops round with a log on our toes.

For fourteen long years I have ser-vi-ed,
And for fourteen long years and a day,
For meeting a bloke in the area,
And sneaking his ticker away.

Oh had I the wings of a turtle-dove,
I'd soar on my pinions so high,
Slap bang to the arms of my Polly love,
And in her sweet presence I'd die.

Now, all my young Dook-ies and Duch-ess-es,
Take warning from what I've to say —
Mind all is your own as you touch-es-es,
Or you'll meet us in Botany Bay.

ANON.

*rum culls* drinking companions ('cull' also has the sense of 'rogue', and 'rum' of 'disreputable')

# The Wild Colonial Boy

'Tis of a wild Colonial boy, Jack Doolan was his name,
Of poor but honest parents he was born in Castlemaine.
He was his father's only hope, his mother's only joy,
And dearly did his parents love the wild Colonial boy.

*Chorus:*
Come, all my hearties, we'll roam the mountains high,
Together we will plunder, together we will die.
We'll wander over valleys, and gallop over plains,
And we'll scorn to live in slavery, bound down with iron chains.

He was scarcely sixteen years of age when he left
his father's home,
And through Australia's sunny clime a bushranger did roam.
He robbed those wealthy squatters, their stock he did destroy,
And a terror to Australia was the wild Colonial boy.

In sixty-one this daring youth commenced his wild career,
With a heart that knew no danger, no foeman did he fear.
He stuck up the Beechworth mail-coach, and robbed
Judge MacEvoy,
Who trembled, and gave up his gold to the wild Colonial boy.

He bade the judge 'Good morning', and told him to beware,
That he'd never rob a hearty chap that acted on the square,
And never to rob a mother of her son and only joy,
Or else you may turn outlaw, like the wild Colonial boy.

One day as he was riding the mountain-side along,
A-listening to the little birds, their pleasant laughing song,
Three mounted troopers rode along — Kelly, Davis,
and FitzRoy —
They thought that they would capture him, the wild
Colonial boy.

'Surrender now, Jack Doolan, you see there's three to one.
Surrender now, Jack Doolan, you daring highwayman.'
He drew a pistol from his belt and shook the little toy.
'I'll fight, but not surrender,' said the wild Colonial boy.

He fired at Trooper Kelly and brought him to the ground,
And in return from Davis received a mortal wound.
All shattered through the jaws he lay still firing at FitzRoy,
And that's the way they captured him — the wild Colonial boy.

ANON.

# The Overlander

There's a trade you all know well —
It's bringing cattle over —
I'll tell you all about the time
When I became a drover.
I made up my mind to try the spec,
To the Clarence I did wander,
And bought a mob of duffers there
To begin as an overlander.

*Chorus:*
Pass the wine cup round, my boys;
Don't let the bottle stand there,
For tonight we'll drink the health
Of every overlander.

When the cattle were all mustered,
And the outfit ready to start,
I saw the lads all mounted,
With their swags left in the cart.
All kinds of men I had
From France, Germany, and Flanders;
Lawyers, doctors, good and bad,
In the mob of overlanders.

From the road I then fed out
When the grass was green and young;
When a squatter with curse and shout
Told me to move along.
I said, 'You're very hard;
Take care, don't raise my dander,

For I'm a regular knowing card,
The Queensland overlander.'

'Tis true we pay no licence,
And our run is rather large;
'Tis not often they catch us,
So they cannot make a charge.
They think we live on store beef,
But no, I'm not a gander;
When a good fat stranger joins the mob,
'He'll do,' says the overlander.

One day a squatter rode up.
Says he, 'You're on my run;
I've got two boys as witnesses,
Consider your stock in pound.'
I tried to coax, thence bounce him,
But my tin I had to squander,
For he put threepence a head
On the mob of the overlander.

The pretty girls in Brisbane
Were hanging out their duds.
I wished to have a chat with them,
So steered straight for the tubs.
Some dirty urchins saw me,
And soon they raised my dander,
Crying, 'Mother, quick! take in the clothes,
Here comes an overlander!'

In town we drain the wine cup,
And go to see the play,
And never think to be hard up

For how to pass the day.
Each has a sweetheart there,
Dressed out in all her grandeur —
Dark eyes and jet black flowing hair,
'She's a plum,' says the overlander.

ANON.

# The Banks of the Condamine

Oh, hark the dogs are barking, love,
I can no longer stay,
The men are all gone mustering
And it is nearly day.
And I must off by the morning light
Before the sun doth shine,
To meet the Sydney shearers
On the banks of the Condamine.

Oh Willie, dearest Willie,
I'll go along with you,
I'll cut off all my auburn fringe
And be a shearer, too,
I'll cook and count your tally, love,
While ringer-o you shine,
And I'll wash your greasy moleskins
On the banks of the Condamine.

Oh, Nancy, dearest Nancy,
With me you cannot go,
The squatters have given orders, love,
No woman should do so;
Your delicate constitution
Is not equal unto mine,
To stand the constant tigering
On the banks of the Condamine.

Oh Willie, dearest Willie,
Then stay back home with me,
We'll take up a selection

And a farmer's wife I'll be:
I'll help you husk the corn, love,
And cook your meals so fine
You'll forget the ram-stag mutton
On the banks of the Condamine.

Oh, Nancy, dearest Nancy,
Please do not hold me back,
Down there the boys are waiting,
And I must be on the track;

So here's a good-bye kiss, love,
Back home here I'll incline
When we've shore the last of the jumbucks
On the banks of the Condamine.

ANON.

*ringer* the shearer with the highest tally
*tigering* strenuous work, 'roughing it'
*ram-stag* a ram castrated after reaching maturity

# Stringybark and Greenhide

I sing of a commodity, it's one that will not fail yer,
I mean the common oddity, the mainstay of Australia;
Gold it is a precious thing, for commerce it increases,
But stringybark and greenhide can beat it all to pieces.

*Chorus:*
Stringybark and greenhide,
That will never fail yer!
Stringybark and greenhide,
The mainstay of Australia.

If you travel on the road and chance to stick in Bargo,
To avoid a bad capsize you must unload your cargo;
For to pull your dray about I do not see the force on,
Take a bit of greenhide and hook another horse on.

If you chance to take a dray, and break your leader's traces,
Get a bit of greenhide to mend your broken places;
Greenhide is a useful thing, all that you require,
But stringybark's another thing, when you want a fire.

If you want to build a hut to keep out wind and weather
Stringybark will make it snug and keep it well together;
Greenhide, if it's used by you, will make it all the stronger,
For if you tie it with greenhide it's sure to last the longer.

New chums to this golden land, never dream of failure,
While you've got such useful things as these in fair Australia;
For stringybark and greenhide will never, never fail yer,
Stringybark and greenhide is the mainstay of Australia.

George Chanson (?)

# The Old Bullock Dray

Now the shearing is all over and the wool is coming down,
I mean to get a wife, me boys, when I go to town,
For everything has got a mate that brings itself to view
From the little paddymelon to the big kangaroo.

*Chorus:*
So roll up your bundle and let us make a push,
And I'll take you up the country and show you the bush;
I'll be bound such a chance you won't get another day,
So roll up and take possession of the old bullock dray.

I'll teach you the whip, and the bullocks how to flog,
You'll be my offsider when I'm fast in the bog,
Hitting out both left and right and every other way,
Making skin, blood and hair fly around the bullock dray.

Good beef and damper, of that you'll get enough,
When boiling in the bucket such a walloper of duff;
My mates, they'll all dance and sing upon our wedding day
To the music of the bells around the old bullock dray.

There'll be lots of piccaninnies, you must remember that,
There'll be 'Buckjumping' Maggie and 'Leather-belly' Pat,
There'll be 'Stringybark' Peggy and 'Green-eyed' Mike,
Yes, my colonial, as many as you like.

Now that I am married and have piccaninnies three,
No one lives so happy as my little wife and me;
She goes out hunting to while away the day
While I take down the wool in the old bullock dray.

ANON.

*paddymelon* small type of wallaby
*offsider* assistant to the bullock-driver, walking on the offside of the team
*my colonial* abbreviation of 'my colonial oath'

# Click Go The Shears

Out on the board the old shearer stands,
Grasping his shears in his long, bony hands,
Fixed is his gaze on a bare-bellied 'joe',
Glory if he gets her, won't he make the ringer go.

*Chorus:*
Click go the shears boys, click, click, click,
Wide is his blow and his hands move quick,
The ringer looks around and is beaten by a blow,
And curses the old snagger with the blue-bellied 'joe'.

In the middle of the floor in his cane-bottomed chair
Is the boss of the board, with eyes everywhere;
Notes well each fleece as it comes to the screen,
Paying strict attention if it's taken off clean.

The colonial-experience man, he is there, of course,
With his shiny leggin's, just got off his horse,
Casting round his eye like a real connoisseur,
Whistling the old tune, 'I'm the Perfect Lure'.

Now Mister Newchum for to begin,
In number seven paddock bring all the sheep in;
Don't leave none behind, whatever you may do,
And then you'll be fit for a jackeroo.

The tar-boy is there, awaiting in demand,
With his blackened tar-pot, and his tarry hand;
Sees one old sheep with a cut upon its back,
Hears what he's waiting for, 'Tar here, Jack!'

Shearing is all over and we've all got our cheques,
Roll up your swag for we're off on the tracks;
The first pub we come to, it's there we'll have a spree,
And everyone that comes along it's, 'Come and drink with me!'

Down by the bar the old shearer stands,
Grasping his glass in his thin bony hands;
Fixed is his gaze on a green-painted keg,
Glory, he'll get down on it, ere he stirs a peg.

There we leave him standing, shouting for all hands,
Whilst all around him every 'shouter' stands;
His eyes are on the cask, which is now lowering fast,
He works hard, he drinks hard, and goes to hell at last!

ANON.

*board* the floor of the woolshed where the shearing is done
*bare-bellied* a bare-bellied sheep is easier to shear
*joe* ewe
*ringer* the shearer with the highest tally in the shed
*blow* the stroke of the shears
*boss of the board* the supervisor, usually the shearing contractor
*colonial-experience man* a young Englishman of good connections sent out to get experience in the colonies

# Flash Jack from Gundagai

I've shore at Burrabogie, and I've shore at Toganmain,
I've shore at big Willandra and upon the old Coleraine,
But before the shearin' was over I've wished myself back again
Shearin' for old Tom Patterson, on the One-Tree Plain.

*Chorus:*
All among the wool, boys,
Keep your wide blades full, boys,
I can do a respectable tally myself whenever I like to try,
But they know me round the backblocks as Flash Jack
from Gundagai.

I've shore at big Willandra and I've shore at Tilberoo,
And once I drew my blades, my boys, upon the famed Barcoo,
At Cowan Downs and Trida, as far as Moulamein,
But I always was glad to get back again to the One-Tree Plain.

I've pinked 'em with the Wolseleys and I've rushed
with B-bows, too,
And shaved 'em in the grease, my boys, with the grass seed
showing through.
But I never slummed my pen, my lads, whate'er it
might contain,
While shearin' for old Tom Patterson, on the One-Tree Plain.

I've been whalin' up the Lachlan, and I've dossed on
    Cooper's Creek,
And once I rung Cudjingie shed, and blued it in a week.
But when Gabriel blows his trumpet, lads, I'll catch the
    morning train,
And I'll push for old Tom Patterson's on the One-Tree Plain.

ANON.

*pinked* to 'pink' is to shear so closely that the skin shows through
*Wolseleys* machine shears, named after their inventor
*B-bows* hand shears
*whalin' up the Lachlan* the 'whalers' were the swagmen who followed the inland rivers, camping and fishing in the bends of the river
*rung Cudjingie shed* achieved the highest tally

# The Dying Stockman

A strapping young stockman lay dying,
His saddle supporting his head;
His two mates around him were crying,
As he rose on his elbow and said:

*Chorus:*
'Wrap me up with my stockwhip and blanket,
And bury me deep down below,
Where the dingoes and crows can't molest me,
In the shade where the coolibahs grow.

'Oh! had I the flight of the bronzewing,
Far o'er the plains would I fly,
Straight to the land of my childhood,
And there I would lay down and die.

'Then cut down a couple of saplings,
Place one at my head and my toe,
Carve on them cross, stockwhip, and saddle,
To show there's a stockman below.

'Hark! there's the wail of a dingo,
Watchful and weird — I must go,
For it tolls the death-knell of the stockman
From the gloom of the scrub down below.

'There's tea in the battered old billy;
Place the pannikins out in a row,
And we'll drink to the next merry meeting,
In the place where all good fellows go.

'And oft in the shades of the twilight,
When the soft winds are whispering low,
And the darkening shadows are falling,
Sometimes think of the stockman below.'

ANON.

# A Mid-summer Noon in the Australian Forest

Not a bird disturbs the air.
There is quiet everywhere;
Over plains and over woods
What a mighty stillness broods.

Even the grasshoppers keep
Where the coolest shadows sleep;
Even the busy ants are found
Resting in their pebbled mound;
Even the locust clingeth now
In silence to the barky bough;
And over hills and over plains
Quiet, vast and slumbrous, reigns.

Only there's a drowsy humming
From yon warm lagoon slow coming:
'Tis the dragon-hornet — see!

All bedaubed resplendently
With yellow on a tawny ground
Each rich spot nor square nor round.
But rudely heart-shaped, as it were
The blurred and hasty impress there.
Of a vermeil-crusted seal
Dusted o'er with golden meal:
Only there's a droning where
Yon bright beetle gleams the air
Gleams it in its droning flight
With a slanting track of light,
Till rising in the sunshine higher,
Its shards flame out like gems on fire.

Every other thing is still,
Save the ever wakeful rill,
Whose cool murmur only throws
A cooler comfort round Repose;
Or some ripple in the sea
Of leafy boughs, where, lazily,
Tired Summer in her forest bower
Turning with the noontide hour,
Heaves a slumbrous breath, ere she
Once more slumbers peacefully.

O 'tis easeful here to lie
Hidden from Noon's scorching eye,
In this grassy cool recess
Musing thus of Quietness.

CHARLES HARPUR

# The Sick Stockrider

Hold hard, Ned! Lift me down once more, and lay me
in the shade.
Old man, you've had your work cut out to guide
Both horses, and to hold me in the saddle when I sway'd
All through the hot, slow, sleepy, silent ride.
The dawn at 'Moorabinda' was a mist rack dull and dense,
The sunrise was a sullen, sluggish lamp;
I was dozing in the gateway at Arbuthnot's bound'ry fence,
I was dreaming on the Limestone cattle camp.

We crossed the creek at Carricksford, and sharply through
the haze,
And suddenly the sun shot flaming forth;
To southward lay 'Katawa' with the sand peaks all ablaze
And the flush'd fields of Glen Lomond lay to north.
Now westward winds the bridle path that leads to Lindisfarm,
And yonder looms the double-headed Bluff;
From the far side of the first hill, when the skies are clear
and calm,
You can see Sylvester's woolshed fair enough.

Five miles we used to call it from our homestead to the place
Where the big tree spans the roadway like an arch;
'Twas here we ran the dingo down that gave us such a chase
Eight years ago — or was it nine? — last March.
'Twas merry in the glowing morn, among the gleaming grass
To wander as we've wandered many a mile,
And blow the cool tobacco cloud, and watch the white
wreaths pass,
Sitting loosely in the saddle all the while.

'Twas merry mid the blackwoods when we spied the station roofs,
To wheel the wild scrub cattle at the yard,
With a running fire of stockwhips and a fiery run of hoofs;
Oh! the hardest day was never then too hard!
Ay! we had a glorious gallop after 'Starlight' and his gang,
When they bolted from Sylvester's on the flat;
How the sun-dried reed-beds crackled, how the flint-strewn ranges rang
To the strokes of 'Mountaineer' and 'Acrobat'!

Hard behind them in the timber, harder still across the heath,
Close beside them through the tea-tree scrub we dash'd;
And the golden-tinted fern leaves, how they rustled underneath!
And the honeysuckle osiers, how they crash'd!
We led the hunt throughout, Ned, on the chestnut and the grey,
And the troopers were three hundred yards behind,
While we emptied our six-shooters on the bushrangers at bay,
In the creek with stunted box-tree for a blind!

There you grappled with the leader, man to man and horse to horse,
And you roll'd together when the chestnut rear'd;
He blazed away and missed you in that shallow water course —
A narrow shave — his powder singed your beard!
In these hours when life is ebbing, how those days when life was young
Come back to us; how clearly I recall
Even the yarns Jack Hall invented, and the songs Jem Roper sung;
And where are now Jem Roper and Jack Hall?

Ay! nearly all our comrades of the old colonial school,
Our ancient boon companions, Ned, are gone;

Hard livers for the most part, somewhat reckless as a rule,
  It seems that you and I are left alone.
There was Hughes, who got in trouble through that business
    with the cards,
  It matters little what became of him;
But a steer ripp'd up Macpherson in the Cooraminta yards,
  And Sullivan was drown'd at Sink-or-Swim.

And Mostyn — poor Frank Mostyn — died at last a fearful
    wreck,
  In the horrors at the Upper Wandinong,
And Carisbrooke, the rider, at the Horsefall broke his neck,
  Faith! the wonder was he saved his neck so long!
Ah! those days and nights we squandered at the Logans'
    in the glen —
  The Logans, man and wife, have long been dead.
Elsie's tallest girl seems taller than your little Elsie then;
  And Ethel is a woman grown and wed.

I've had my share of pastime, and I've done my share of toil,
  And life is short — the longest life a span;
I care not now to tarry for the corn or for the oil,
  Or for the wine that maketh glad the heart of man.
For good undone and gifts misspent and resolutions vain,
  'Tis somewhat late to trouble. This I know —
I should live the same life over, if I had to live again;
  And the chances are I go where most men go.

The deep blue skies wax dusky and the tall green
    trees grow dim,
  The sward beneath me seems to heave and fall;
And sickly, smoky shadows through the sleepy sunlight swim,
  And on the very sun's face weave their pall.

Let me slumber in the hollow where the wattle blossoms wave,
  With never stone or rail to fence my bed;
Should the sturdy station children pull the bush flowers
    on my grave,
  I may chance to hear them romping overhead.

ADAM LINDSAY GORDON

## *From: Ye Wearie Wayfarer*

---

'Question not, but live and labour
  Till yon goal be won,
Helping every feeble neighbour,
  Seeking help from none;
Life is mostly froth and bubble,
  Two things stand like stone:
KINDNESS in another's trouble,
  COURAGE in your own.'

ADAM LINDSAY GORDON

# Where the Dead Men Lie

Out on the wastes of the Never Never —
  That's where the dead men lie!
There where the heat-waves dance for ever —
  That's where the dead men lie!
That's where the Earth's loved sons are keeping
Endless tryst: not the west wind sweeping
Feverish pinions can wake their sleeping —
  Out where the dead men lie!

Where brown Summer and Death have mated —
  That's where the dead men lie!
Loving with fiery lust unsated —
  That's where the dead men lie!
Out where the grinning skulls bleach whitely
Under the saltbush sparkling brightly;
Out where the wild dogs chorus nightly —
  That's where the dead men lie!

Deep in the yellow, flowing river —
  That's where the dead men lie!
Under the banks where the shadows quiver -
  That's where the dead men lie!
Where the platypus twists and doubles,
Leaving a train of tiny bubbles;
Rid at last of their earthly troubles —
  That's where the dead men lie!

East and backward pale faces turning —
  That's how the dead men lie!
Gaunt arms stretched with a voiceless yearning —

That's how the dead men lie!
Oft in the fragrant hush of nooning
Hearing again their mother's crooning,
Wrapt for aye in a dreamful swooning —
That's how the dead men lie!

Only the hand of Night can free them —
That's when the dead men fly!
Only the frightened cattle see them —
See the dead men go by!
Cloven hoofs beating out one measure,
Bidding the stockmen know no leisure —
That's when the dead men take their pleasure!
That's when the dead men fly!

Ask, too, the never-sleeping drover:
He sees the dead pass by;
Hearing them call to their friends — the plover,
Hearing the dead men cry;
Seeing their faces stealing, stealing,
Hearing their laughter, pealing, pealing,
Watching their grey forms wheeling, wheeling
Round where the cattle lie!

Strangled by thirst and fierce privation —
That's how the dead men die!
Out on Moneygrub's farthest station —
That's how the dead men die!
Hard-faced greybeards, youngsters callow;
Some mounds cared for, some left fallow;
Some deep down, yet others shallow;
Some having but the sky.

Moneygrub, as he sips his claret,
  Looks with complacent eye
Down at his watch-chain, eighteen carat —
  There, in his club, hard by:
Recks not that every link is stamped with
Names of the men whose limbs are cramped with
Too long lying in grave-mould, cramped with
  Death where the dead men lie.

BARCROFT BOAKE

*Never Never* the regions remote from settlement

# The Women of the West

They left the vine-wreathed cottage and the mansion
  on the hill,
The houses in the busy streets where life is never still,
The pleasures of the city, and the friends they cherished best:
For love they faced the wilderness — the Women of the West.

The roar, and rush, and fever of the city died away,
And the old-time joys and faces — they were gone for
  many a day;
In their place the lurching coach-wheel, or the creaking
  bullock chains,
O'er the everlasting sameness of the never-ending plains.

In the slab-built, zinc-roofed homestead of some
lately-taken run,
In the tent beside the bankment of a railway just begun,
In the huts on new selections, in the camps of man's unrest,
On the frontiers of the Nation, live the Women of the West.

The red sun robs their beauty, and, in weariness and pain,
The slow years steal the nameless grace that never
comes again;
And there are hours men cannot soothe, and words men
cannot say —
The nearest woman's face may be a hundred miles away.

The wide Bush holds the secrets of their longings and desires,
When the white stars in reverence light their holy altar-fires,
And silence, like the touch of God, sinks deep into the breast —
Perchance He hears and understands the Women of the West.

For them no trumpet sounds the call, no poet plies his arts —
They only hear the beating of their gallant, loving hearts.
But they have sung with silent lives the song all songs above —
The holiness of sacrifice, the dignity of love.

Well have we held our father's creed. No call has passed us by.
We faced and fought the wilderness, we sent our sons to die.
And we have hearts to do and dare, and yet, o'er all the rest,
The hearts that made the Nation were the Women of the West.

G. Essex Evans

# The Last of His Tribe

He crouches, and buries his face on his knees,
And hides in the dark of his hair;
For he cannot look up to the storm-smitten trees,
Or think of the loneliness there —
Of the loss and the loneliness there.

The wallaroos grope through the tufts of the grass,
And turn to their coverts for fear;
But he sits in the ashes and lets them pass
Where the boomerangs sleep with the spear —
With the nullah, the sling, and the spear.

Uloola, behold him! The thunder that breaks
On the tops of the rocks with the rain,
And the wind which drives up with the salt of the lakes,
Have made him a hunter again —
A hunter and fisher again.

For his eyes have been full with a smouldering thought;
But he dreams of the hunts of yore,
And of foes that he sought, and of fights that he fought
With those who will battle no more —
Who will go to the battle no more.

It is well that the water which tumbles and fills
Goes moaning and moaning along;
For an echo rolls out from the sides of the hills,
And he starts at a wonderful song —
At the sound of a wonderful song.

And he sees through the rents of the scattering fogs
The corroboree warlike and grim,
And the lubra who sat by the fire on the logs,
To watch, like a mourner, for him —
Like a mother and mourner for him.

Will he go in his sleep from these desolate lands,
Like a chief, to the rest of his race,
With the honey-voiced woman who beckons and stands,
And gleams like a dream in his face —
Like a marvellous dream in his face?

HENRY KENDALL

# Song of the Cattle-hunters

While the morning light beams on the fern-matted streams,
And the water-pools flash in its glow,
Down the ridges we fly, with a loud ringing cry —
Down the ridges and gullies we go!
And the cattle we hunt, they are racing in front,
With a roar like the thunder of waves;
As the beat and the beat of our swift horses' feet
Start the echoes away from their caves!
As the beat and the beat
Of our swift horses' feet
Start the echoes away from their caves!

Like a wintery shore that the waters ride o'er,
All the lowlands are filling with sound;
For swiftly we gain where the herds on the plain,
Like a tempest, are tearing the ground!
And we'll follow them hard to the rails of the yard,
Over gulches and mountain-tops grey,
Where the beat and the beat of our swift horses' feet
Will die with the echoes away!
Where the beat and the beat
Of our swift horses' feet
Will die with the echoes away!

HENRY KENDALL

# *Bell-birds*

By channels of coolness the echoes are calling,
And down the dim gorges I hear the creek falling;
It lives in the mountain, where moss and the sedges
Touch with their beauty the banks and the ledges;
Through brakes of the cedar and sycamore bowers
Struggles the light that is love to the flowers.
And, softer than slumber, and sweeter than singing,
The notes of the bell-birds are running and ringing.

The silver-voiced bell-birds, the darlings of day-time,
They sing in September their songs of the May-time.
When shadows wax strong, and the thunder-bolts hurtle,
They hide with their fear in the leaves of the myrtle;
When rain and the sunbeams shine mingled together
They start up like fairies that follow fair weather,
And straightway the hues of their feathers unfolden
Are the green and the purple, the blue and the golden.

October, the maiden of bright yellow tresses,
Loiters for love in these cool wildernesses;
Loiters knee-deep in the grasses to listen,
Where dripping rocks gleam and the leafy pools glisten.
Then is the time when the water-moons splendid
Break with their gold, and are scattered or blended
Over the creeks, till the woodlands have warning
Of songs of the bell-bird and wings of the morning.

Welcome as waters unkissed by the summers
Are the voices of bell-birds to thirsty far-comers.
When fiery December sets foot in the forest,

And the need of the wayfarer presses the sorest,
Pent in the ridges for ever and ever,
The bell-birds direct him to spring and to river,
With ring and with ripple, like runnels whose torrents
Are toned by the pebbles and leaves in the currents.

Often I sit, looking back to a childhood
Mixt with the sights and the sounds of the wildwood,
Longing for power and the sweetness to fashion
Lyrics with beats like the heart-beats of passion —
Songs interwoven of lights and of laughters
Borrowed from bell-birds in far forest rafters;
*So* I might keep in the city and alleys
The beauty and strength of the deep mountain valleys,
Charming to slumber the pain of my losses
With glimpses of creeks and a vision of mosses.

HENRY KENDALL

# A Bushman's Song

I'm travellin' down the Castlereagh, and I'm a station-hand,
I'm handy with the ropin' pole, I'm handy with the brand,
And I can ride a rowdy colt, or swing the axe all day,
But there's no demand for a station-hand along the Castlereagh.

So it's shift, boys, shift, for there isn't the slightest doubt
That we've got to make a shift to the stations further out,

With the packhorse runnin' after, for he follows like a dog,
We must strike across the country at the old jig-jog.

This old black horse I'm riding — if you'll notice what's
his brand,
He wears the crooked R, you see — none better in the land.
He takes a lot of beatin', and the other day we tried,
For a bit of a joke, with a racing bloke, for twenty pounds
a side.

It was shift, boys, shift, for there wasn't the slightest doubt
That I had to make him shift, for the money was further out;
But he cantered home a winner, with the other one at
the flog —
He's a red-hot sort to pick up with his old jig-jog.

I asked a cove for shearin' once along the Marthaguy:
'We shear non-union here,' says he. 'I call it scab,' says I.
I looked along the shearin' floor before I turned to go —
There were eight or ten dashed Chinamen a-shearin' in a row.

It was shift, boys, shift, for there wasn't the slightest doubt
It was time to make a shift with the leprosy about.
So I saddled up my horses, and I whistled to my dog,
And I left his scabby station at the old jig-jog.

I went to Illawarra, where my brother's got a farm;
He has to ask his landlord's leave before he lifts his arm;
The landlord owns the countryside — man, woman, dog,
and cat,
They haven't the cheek to dare to speak without they touch
their hat.

It was shift, boys, shift, for there wasn't the slightest doubt
Their little landlord god and I would soon have fallen out;
Was I to touch my hat to him? — was I his bloomin' dog?
So I makes for up the country at the old jig-jog.

A. B. PATERSON

# *Waltzing Matilda*

Oh! there once was a swagman camped in a billabong,
Under the shade of a coolibah-tree;
And he sang as he looked at his old billy boiling,
'Who'll come a-waltzing Matilda with me?'

*Chorus:*
Who'll come a-waltzing Matilda, my darling,
Who'll come a-waltzing Matilda with me?
Waltzing Matilda and leading a water-bag —
Who'll come a-waltzing Matilda with me?

Down came a jumbuck to drink at the water-hole,
Up jumped the swagman and grabbed him in glee;
And he sang as he stowed him away in his tucker-bag,
'You'll come a-waltzing Matilda with me!'

Down came the squatter a-riding his thoroughbred;
Down came policemen — one, two, and three.
'Whose is the jumbuck you've got in the tucker-bag?
You'll come a-waltzing Matilda with me.'

But the swagman he up and he jumped in the water-hole,
Drowning himself by the coolibah-tree;
And his ghost may be heard as it sings in the billabong,
'Who'll come a-waltzing Matilda with me?'

A. B. PATERSON

# The Man from Snowy River

There was movement at the station, for the word had passed around
That the colt from old Regret had got away,
And had joined the wild bush horses — he was worth a thousand pound,
So all the cracks had gathered to the fray.
All the tried and noted riders from the stations near and far
Had mustered at the homestead overnight,
For the bushmen love hard riding where the wild bush horses are,
And the stock horse snuffs the battle with delight.

There was Harrison, who made his pile when Pardon won the cup,
The old man with his hair as white as snow;
But few could ride beside him when his blood was fairly up —
He would go wherever horse and man could go.

And Clancy of the Overflow came down to lend a hand,
No better horseman ever held the reins;
For never horse could throw him while the saddle girths
would stand,
He learnt to ride while droving on the plains.

And one was there, a stripling on a small and weedy beast,
He was something like a racehorse undersized,
With a touch of Timor pony — three parts thoroughbred
at least —
And such as are by mountain horsemen prized.
He was hard and tough and wiry — just the sort that won't
say die —
There was courage in his quick impatient tread;
And he bore the badge of gameness in his bright and fiery eye,
And the proud and lofty carriage of his head.

But still so slight and weedy, one would doubt his power to stay,
And the old man said, 'That horse will never do
For a long and tiring gallop — lad, you'd better stop away,
Those hills are far too rough for such as you.'
So he waited sad and wistful — only Clancy stood his friend —
'I think we ought to let him come,' he said;
'I warrant he'll be with us when he's wanted at the end,
For both his horse and he are mountain bred.

'He hails from Snowy River, up by Kosciusko's side,
Where the hills are twice as steep and twice as rough,
Where a horse's hoofs strike firelight from the flint stones
every stride,
The man that holds his own is good enough.

And the Snowy River riders on the mountains make their home,
Where the river runs those giant hills between;
I have seen full many horsemen since I first commenced
to roam,
But nowhere yet such horsemen have I seen.'

So he went — they found the horses by the big
mimosa clump —
They raced away towards the mountain's brow,
And the old man gave his orders, 'Boys, go at them from
the jump,
No use to try for fancy riding now.
And, Clancy, you must wheel them, try and wheel them to
the right
Ride boldly, lad, and never fear the spills,
For never yet was rider that could keep the mob in sight,
If once they gain the shelter of those hills.'

So Clancy rode to wheel them — he was racing on the wing
Where the best and boldest riders take their place,
And he raced his stockhorse past them, and he made
the ranges ring
With the stockwhip, as he met them face to face.
Then they halted for a moment, while he swung the
dreaded lash,
But they saw their well-loved mountain full in view,
And they charged beneath the stockwhip with a sharp and
sudden dash,
And off into the mountain scrub they flew.

Then fast the horsemen followed, where the gorges deep
and black
Resounded to the thunder of their tread,

And the stockwhips woke the echoes, and they fiercely
answered back
From cliffs and crags that beetled overhead.
And upward, ever upward, the wild horses held their way,
Where mountain ash and kurrajong grew wide;
And the old man muttered fiercely, 'We may bid the mob
good day,
*No* man can hold them down the other side.'

When they reached the mountain's summit, even Clancy
took a pull,
It might well make the boldest hold their breath,
The wild hop scrub grew thickly, and the hidden ground was full
Of wombat holes, and any slip was death.
But the man from Snowy River let the pony have his head,
And he swung his stockwhip round and gave a cheer,
And he raced him down the mountain like a torrent
down its bed,
While the others stood and watched in very fear.

He sent the flint stones flying, but the pony kept his feet,
He cleared the fallen timber in his stride,
And the man from Snowy River never shifted in his seat —
It was grand to see that mountain horseman ride.
Through the stringybarks and saplings, on the rough and
broken ground,
Down the hillside at a racing pace he went;
And he never drew the bridle till he landed safe and sound,
At the bottom of that terrible descent.

He was right among the horses as they climbed the further hill,
And the watchers on the mountain standing mute,
Saw him ply the stockwhip fiercely, he was right among
them still,

As he raced across the clearing in pursuit.
Then they lost him for a moment, where two mountain
    gullies met
In the ranges, but a final glimpse reveals
On a dim and distant hillside the wild horses racing yet,
With the man from Snowy River at their heels.

And he ran them single-handed till their sides were white
    with foam.
He followed like a bloodhound on their track,
Till they halted cowed and beaten, then he turned their heads
    for home,
And alone and unassisted brought them back.
But his hardy mountain pony could scarcely raise a trot,
He was blood from hip to shoulder from the spur;
But his pluck was still undaunted, and his courage fiery hot,
For never yet was mountain horse a cur.

And down by Kosciusko, where the pine-clad ridges raise
Their torn and rugged battlements on high,
Where the air is clear as crystal, and the white stars fairly blaze
At midnight in the cold and frosty sky,
And where around The Overflow the reed beds sweep and sway
To the breezes, and the rolling plains are wide,
The man from Snowy River is a household word today,
And the stockmen tell the story of his ride.

A. B. PATERSON

# Clancy of The Overflow

I had written him a letter which I had, for want of better
Knowledge, sent to where I met him down the Lachlan,
years ago;
He was shearing when I knew him, so I sent the letter to him,
Just 'on spec', addressed as follows: 'Clancy, of The Overflow'.

And an answer came directed in a writing unexpected,
(And I think the same was written with a thumbnail dipped
in tar);
'Twas his shearing mate who wrote it, and *verbatim* I will
quote it:
'Clancy's gone to Queensland droving, and we don't know
where he are.'

* * * *

In my wild erratic fancy visions come to me of Clancy
Gone a-droving 'down the Cooper' where the Western
drovers go;
As the stock are slowly stringing, Clancy rides behind
them singing,
For the drover's life has pleasures that the townsfolk
never know.

And the bush hath friends to meet him, and their kindly voices
greet him
In the murmur of the breezes and the river on its bars,
And he sees the vision splendid of the sunlit plains extended,
And at night the wondrous glory of the everlasting stars.

* * * *

I am sitting in my dingy little office, where a stingy
Ray of sunlight struggles feebly down between the houses tall,
And the foetid air and gritty of the dusty, dirty city
Through the open window floating, spreads its foulness over all.

And in place of lowing cattle, I can hear the fiendish rattle
Of the tramways and the buses making hurry down the street,
And the language uninviting of the gutter children fighting
Comes fitfully and faintly through the ceaseless tramp of feet.

And the hurrying people daunt me, and their pallid faces haunt me
As they shoulder one another in their rush and nervous haste,
With their eager eyes and greedy, and their stunted forms and weedy,
For townsfolk have no time to grow, they have no time to waste.

And I somehow rather fancy that I'd like to change with Clancy,
Like to take a turn at droving where the seasons come and go,
While he faced the round eternal of the cashbook and the journal —
But I doubt he'd suit the office, Clancy, of 'The Overflow'.

A. B. PATERSON

# Saltbush Bill

Now this is the law of the Overland that all in the West obey,
A man must cover with travelling sheep a six-mile stage a day;
But this is the law which the drovers make, right easily understood,
They travel their stage where the grass is bad, but they camp where the grass is good;
They camp, and they ravage the squatter's grass till never a blade remains,
Then they drift away as the white clouds drift on the edge of the saltbush plains.
From camp to camp and from run to run they battle it hand to hand,
For a blade of grass and the right to pass on the track of the Overland.

For this is the law of the Great Stock Routes, 'tis written in white and black —
The man that goes with a travelling mob must keep to a half-mile track;
And the drovers keep to a half-mile track on the runs where the grass is dead,
But they spread their sheep on a well-grassed run till they go with a two-mile spread.
So the squatters hurry the drovers on from dawn till the fall of night,
And the squatters' dogs and the drovers' dogs get mixed in a deadly fight;
Yet the squatters' men, though they hunt the mob, are willing the peace to keep,

For the drovers learn how to use their hands when they go with
the travelling sheep;
But this is the tale of a Jackaroo that came from a
foreign strand,
And the fight that he fought with Saltbush Bill, the King of
the Overland.

Now Saltbush Bill was a drover tough, as ever the
country knew,
He had fought his way on the Great Stock Routes from the sea
to the Big Barcoo;
He could tell when he came to a friendly run that gave him a
chance to spread,
And he knew where the hungry owners were that hurried his
sheep ahead;
He was drifting down in the Eighty drought with a mob that
could scarcely creep,
(When the kangaroos by the thousands starve, it is rough on
the travelling sheep.)
And he camped one night at the crossing place on the edge of
the Wilga run,
'We must manage a feed for them here,' he said, 'or the half of
the mob are done!'
So he spread them out when they left the camp wherever they
liked to go,
Till he grew aware of a Jackaroo with a station hand in tow,
And they set to work on the straggling sheep, and with many a
stockwhip crack
They forced them in where the grass was dead in the space of
the half-mile track;
So William prayed that the hand of fate might suddenly strike
him blue
But he'd get some grass for his starving sheep in the teeth of
that Jackaroo.

So he turned and cursed the Jackaroo, he cursed him alive
or dead,
From the soles of his great unwieldy feet to the crown of his
ugly head,
With an extra curse on the moke he rode and the cur at his
heels that ran,
Till the Jackaroo from his horse got down and he went for the
drover man;
With the station hand for his picker-up, though the sheep ran
loose the while,
They battled it out on the saltbush plain in the regular prize
ring style.

Now, the new chum fought for his honour's sake and the pride
of the English race,
But the drover fought for his daily bread with a smile on his
bearded face;
So he shifted ground and he sparred for wind and he made it
a lengthy mill,
And from time to time as his scouts came in they whispered to
Saltbush Bill —
'We have spread the sheep with a two-mile spread, and the
grass it is something grand,
You must stick to him, Bill, for another round for the pride of
the Overland.'

The new chum made it a rushing fight, though never a blow
got home,
Till the sun rode high in the cloudless sky and glared on the
brick-red loam,
Till the sheep drew in to the shelter trees and settled them
down to rest,
Then the drover said he would fight no more and he gave his
opponent best.

So the new chum rode to the homestead straight and he told
them a story grand
Of the desperate fight that he fought that day with the King of
the Overland.
And the tale went home to the public schools of the pluck of the
English swell,
How the drover fought for his very life, but blood in the end
must tell.
But the travelling sheep and the Wilga sheep were boxed on the
Old Man Plain.
'Twas a full week's work ere they drafted out and hunted them
off again,
With a week's good grass in their wretched hides, with a curse
and a stockwhip crack.
They hunted them off on the road once more to starve on the
half-mile track.
And Saltbush Bill, on the Overland, will many a time recite
How the best day's work that he ever did was the day that he
lost the fight.

A. B. PATERSON

# The Man from Ironbark

It was the man from Ironbark who struck the Sydney town,
He wandered over street and park, he wandered up and down.
He loitered here, he loitered there, till he was like to drop,
Until at last in sheer despair he sought a barber's shop.

''Ere! shave my beard and whiskers off, I'll be a man of mark,
I'll go and do the Sydney toff up home in Ironbark.'

The barber man was small and flash, as barbers mostly are,
He wore a strike-your-fancy sash, he smoked a huge cigar;
He was a humorist of note and keen at repartee,
He laid the odds and kept a 'tote', whatever that may be,
And when he saw our friend arrive, he whispered,
'Here's a lark!
Just watch me catch him all alive, this man from Ironbark.'

There were some gilded youths that sat along the barber's wall.
Their eyes were dull, their heads were flat, they had no brains
at all;
To them the barber passed the wink, his dexter eyelid shut,
'I'll make this bloomin' yokel think his bloomin' throat is cut.'
And as he soaped and rubbed it in he made a rude remark:
'I s'pose the flats is pretty green up there in Ironbark.'

A grunt was all reply he got; he shaved the bushman's chin,
Then made the water boiling hot and dipped the razor in.
He raised his hand, his brow grew black, he paused awhile
to gloat,
Then slashed the red-hot razor-back across his victim's throat;
Upon the newly-shaven skin it made a livid mark —
No doubt it fairly took him in — the man from Ironbark.

He fetched a wild up-country yell might wake the dead to hear,
And though his throat, he knew full well, was cut from
ear to ear,
He struggled gamely to his feet, and faced the murd'rous foe:
'You've done for me! you dog, I'm beat! one hit before I go!
I only wish I had a knife, you blessed murdering shark!
But you'll remember all your life the man from Ironbark.'

He lifted up his hairy paw, with one tremendous clout
He landed on the barber's jaw, and knocked the barber out.
He set to work with nail and tooth, he made the place a wreck;
He grabbed the nearest gilded youth, and tried to break
his neck.
And all the while his throat he held to save his vital spark,
And 'Murder! Bloody murder!' yelled the man from Ironbark.

A peelerman who heard the din came in to see the show;
He tried to run the bushman in, but he refused to go.
And when at last the barber spoke, and said ''Twas all in fun —
'Twas just a little harmless joke, a trifle overdone.'
'A joke!' he cried, 'By George, that's fine; a lively sort of lark;
I'd like to catch that murdering swine some night in Ironbark.'

And now while round the shearing floor the list'ning shearers
gape,
He tells the story o'er and o'er, and brags of his escape.
'Them barber chaps what keeps a tote, By George, I've had
enough,
One tried to cut my bloomin' throat, but thank the Lord
it's tough.'
And whether he's believed or no, there's one thing to remark,
That flowing beards are all the go way up in Ironbark.

A. B. PATERSON

# A Bush Christening

On the outer Barcoo where the churches are few,
And men of religion are scanty,
On a road never cross'd 'cept by folk that are lost,
One Michael Magee had a shanty.

Now this Mike was the dad of a ten-year-old lad,
Plump, healthy, and stoutly conditioned;
He was strong as the best, but poor Mike had no rest
For the youngster had never been christened.

And his wife used to cry, 'If the darlin' should die
Saint Peter would not recognise him.'
But by luck he survived till a preacher arrived,
Who agreed straightaway to baptise him.

Now the artful young rogue, while they held their collogue,
With his ear to the keyhole was listenin',
And he muttered in fright while his features turned white,
'What the divil and all is this christenin'?'

He was none of your dolts, he had seen them brand colts,
And it seemed to his small understanding,
If the man in the frock made him one of the flock,
It must mean something very like branding.

So away with a rush he set off for the bush,
While the tears in his eyelids they glistened —
''Tis outrageous,' says he, 'to brand youngsters like me,
I'll be dashed if I'll stop to be christened!'

Like a young native dog he ran into a log,
  And his father with language uncivil,
Never heeding the 'praste' cried aloud in his haste,
  'Come out and be christened, you divil!'

But he lay there as snug as a bug in a rug,
  And his parents in vain might reprove him,
Till his reverence spoke (he was fond of a joke)
  'I've a notion,' says he, 'that'll move him.

'Poke a stick up the log, give the spalpeen a prog;
  Poke him aisy — don't hurt him or maim him,
'Tis not long that he'll stand, I've the water at hand,
  As he rushes out this end I'll name him.

'Here he comes, and for shame! ye've forgotten the name —
  Is it Patsy or Michael or Dinnis?'
Here the youngster ran out, and the priest gave a shout —
  'Take your chance, anyhow, wid 'Maginnis'!'

As the howling young cub ran away to the scrub
  Where he knew that pursuit would be risky,
The priest, as he fled, flung a flask at his head
  That was labelled 'Maginnis's Whisky!'

And Maginnis Magee has been made a J.P.,
  And the one thing he hates more than sin is
To be asked by the folk who have heard of the joke,
  How he came to be christened 'Maginnis'!

A. B. PATERSON

# Been There Before

There came a stranger to Walgett town,
  To Walgett town when the sun was low,
And he carried a thirst that was worth a crown,
  Yet how to quench it he did not know;
But he thought he might take those yokels down,
The guileless yokels of Walgett town.

They made him a bet in a private bar,
  In a private bar when the talk was high,
And they bet him some pounds no matter how far
  He could pelt a stone, yet he could not shy
A stone right over the river so brown,
The Darling River at Walgett town.

He knew that the river from bank to bank
  Was fifty yards, and he smiled a smile
As he trundled down, but his hopes they sank
  For there wasn't a stone within fifty mile;
For the saltbush plain and the open down
Produce no quarries in Walgett town.

The yokels laughed at his hopes o'erthrown,
  And he stood awhile like a man in a dream;
Then out of his pocket he fetched a stone,
  And pelted it over the silent stream —
He had been there before: he had wandered down
On a previous visit to Walgett town.

A. B. Paterson

# The Geebung Polo Club

It was somewhere up the country, in a land of rock and scrub,
That they formed an institution called the Geebung
Polo Club.
They were long and wiry natives from the rugged
mountainside,
And the horse was never saddled that the Geebungs
couldn't ride;
But their style of playing polo was irregular and rash —
They had mighty little science, but a mighty lot of dash:
And they played on mountain ponies that were muscular
and strong,
Though their coats were quite unpolished, and their manes
and tails were long.
And they used to train those ponies wheeling cattle
in the scrub:
They were demons, were the members of the Geebung
Polo Club.

It was somewhere down the country, in a city's smoke
and steam,
That a polo club existed, called the Cuff and Collar Team.
As a social institution 'twas a marvellous success,
For the members were distinguished by exclusiveness
and dress.
They had natty little ponies that were nice, and smooth,
and sleek,
For their cultivated owners only rode 'em once a week.
So they started up the country in pursuit of sport and fame,
For they meant to show the Geebungs how they ought to play
the game;

And they took their valets with them — just to give their boots
a rub
Ere they started operations on the Geebung Polo Club.

Now my readers can imagine how the contest ebbed and flowed,
When the Geebung boys got going it was time to clear the road;
And the game was so terrific that ere half the time was gone
A spectator's leg was broken — just from merely looking on.
For they waddied one another till the plain was strewn
with dead,
While the score was kept so even that they neither got ahead.
And the Cuff and Collar captain, when he tumbled off to die,
Was the last surviving player — so the game was called a tie.

Then the captain of the Geebungs raised him slowly from
the ground,
Though his wounds were mostly mortal, yet he fiercely
gazed around;
There was no one to oppose him — all the rest were
in a trance,
So he scrambled on his pony for his last expiring chance,
For he meant to make an effort to get victory to his side;
So he struck at goal — and missed it — then he tumbled off
and died.

* * * *

By the old Campaspe River, where the breezes shake the grass,
There's a row of little gravestones that the stockmen
never pass,
For they bear a crude inscription saying, 'Stranger, drop a tear,
For the Cuff and Collar players and the Geebung boys lie here.'
And on misty moonlit evenings, while the dingoes howl around,

You can see their shadows flitting down that phantom
polo ground;
You can hear the loud collisions as the flying players meet,
And the rattle of the mallets, and the rush of ponies' feet,
Till the terrified spectator rides like blazes to the pub —
He's been haunted by the spectres of the Geebung Polo Club.

A. B. PATERSON

# Andy's Gone With Cattle

Our Andy's gone to battle now
'Gainst Drought, the red marauder:
Our Andy's gone with cattle now
Across the Queensland border.

He's left us in dejection now;
Our hearts with him are roving.
It's dull on this selection now,
Since Andy went a-droving.

Who now shall wear the cheerful face
In times when things are slackest?
And who shall whistle round the place
When Fortune frowns her blackest?

O who shall cheek the squatter now
  When he comes round us snarling?
His tongue is growing hotter now
  Since Andy crossed the Darling.

The gates are out of order now,
  In storms the riders rattle;
For far across the border now
  Our Andy's gone with cattle.

Poor Aunty's looking thin and white;
  And Uncle's cross with worry;
And poor old Blucher howls all night
  Since Andy left Macquarie.

O may the showers in torrents fall,
  And all the tanks run over;
And may the grass grow green and tall
  In pathways of the drover.

And may good angels send the rain
  On desert stretches sandy;
And when the summer comes again
  God grant 'twill bring us Andy.

HENRY LAWSON

# The Ballad of the Drover

Across the stony ridges,
  Across the rolling plain,
Young Harry Dale, the drover,
  Comes riding home again.
And well his stock-horse bears him,
  And light of heart is he,
And stoutly his old pack-horse
  Is trotting by his knee.

Up Queensland way with cattle
  He travelled regions vast;
And many months have vanished
  Since home-folk saw him last.
He hums a song of someone
  He hopes to marry soon;
And hobble-chains and camp-ware
  Keep jingling to the tune.

Beyond the hazy dado
  Against the lower skies
And yon blue line of ranges
  The homestead station lies.
And thitherward the drover
  Jogs through the lazy noon,
While hobble-chains and camp-ware
  Are jingling to a tune.

An hour has filled the heavens
  With storm-clouds inky black;
At times the lightning trickles

Around the drover's track;
But Harry pushes onward,
His horses' strength he tries,
In hope to reach the river
Before the flood shall rise.

The thunder from above him
Goes rolling o'er the plain;
And down on thirsty pastures
In torrents falls the rain.
And every creek and gully
Sends forth its little flood,
Till the river runs a banker,
All stained with yellow mud.

Now Harry speaks to Rover,
The best dog on the plains,
And to his hardy horses,
And strokes their shaggy manes:
'We've breasted bigger rivers
When floods were at their height
Nor shall this gutter stop us
From getting home to-night!'

The thunder growls a warning,
The ghastly lightnings gleam,
As the drover turns his horses
To swim the fatal stream.
But O the flood runs stronger
Than e'er it ran before;
The saddle-horse is failing,
And only half-way o'er!

When flashes next the lightning,
The flood's grey breast is blank,

And a cattle dog and pack-horse
  Are struggling up the bank.
But in the lonely homestead
  The girl shall wait in vain —
He'll never pass the stations
  In charge of stock again.

The faithful dog a moment
  Sits panting on the bank,
And then swims through the current
  To where his master sank.
And round and round in circles
  He fights with failing strength,
Till, borne down by the waters,
  The old dog sinks at length.

Across the flooded lowland
  And slopes of sodden loam
The pack-horse struggles onward,
  To take dumb tidings home.
And mud-stained, wet, and weary,
  Through ranges dark goes he;
While hobble-chains and tinware
  Are sounding eerily.

The floods are in the ocean,
  The creeks are clear again,
And now a verdant carpet
  Is stretched across the plain.
But bleaching on the desert
  Or in the river reeds
The bones lie of the bravest
  That wide Australia breeds.

HENRY LAWSON

# The Shearers

No church-bell rings them from the Track,
  No pulpit lights their blindness —
'Tis hardship, drought and homelessness
  That teach those Bushmen kindness:
The mateship born of barren lands,
  Of toil and thirst and danger —
The camp-fare for the stranger set,
  The first place to the stranger.

They do the best they can to-day —
  Take no thought of the morrow;
Their way is not the old-world way —
  They live to lend and borrow.
When shearing's done and cheques gone wrong,
  They call it 'time to slither' —
They saddle up and say 'So-long!'
  And ride — the Lord knows whither.

And though he may be brown or black,
  Or wrong man there or right man,
The mate that's honest to his mates
  They call that man a 'white man'!
They tramp in mateship side by side —
  The Protestant and 'Roman' —
They call no biped lord or 'sir'
  And touch their hats to no man!

They carry in their swags, perhaps,
  A portrait and a letter —
And, maybe, deep down in their hearts,

The hope of 'something better'.
Where lonely miles are long to ride,
And all days seem recurrent,
There's lots of time to think of men
They might have been — but weren't.

They turn their faces to the west
And leave the world behind them —
(Their drought-dried graves are seldom green
Where even mates can find them).
They know too little of the world
To rise to wealth or greatness:
But in this book of mine I pay
My tribute to their straightness.

HENRY LAWSON

# The Teams

A cloud of dust on the long white road,
And the teams go creeping on
Inch by inch with the weary load;
And by the power of the green-hide goad
The distant goal is won.

With eyes half-shut to the blinding dust,
And necks to the yokes bent low,
The beasts are pulling as bullocks must;

And the shining tires might almost rust
  While the spokes are turning slow.

With face half-hid 'neath a broad-brimmed hat
  That shades from the heat's white waves,
And shouldered whip with its green-hide plait,
The driver plods with a gait like that
  Of his weary, patient slaves.

He wipes his brow, for the day is hot,
  And spits to the left with spite;
He shouts at Bally, and flicks at Scot,
And raises dust from the back of Spot,
  And spits to the dusty right.

He'll sometimes pause as a thing of form
  In front of a settler's door,
And ask for a drink, and remark, 'It's warm,'
Or say, 'There's signs of a thunderstorm;'
  But he seldom utters more.

The rains are heavy on roads like these;
  And, fronting his lonely home,
For days together the settler sees
The waggons bogged to the axletrees,
  Or ploughing the sodden loam.

And then when the roads are at their worst,
  The bushman's children hear
The cruel blows of the whips reversed
While bullocks pull as their hearts would burst,
  And bellow with pain and fear.

And thus — with glimpses of home and rest —
Are the long, long journeys done;
And thus — 'tis a thankless life at the best —
Is distance fought in the mighty West,
And the lonely battles won.

HENRY LAWSON

# *Middleton's Rouseabout*

Tall and freckled and sandy,
Face of a country lout;
This was the picture of Andy,
Middleton's Rouseabout.

Type of a coming nation,
In the land of cattle and sheep,
Worked on Middleton's station,
'Pound a week and his keep'.

On Middleton's wide dominions
Plied the stockwhip and shears;
Hadn't any opinions,
Hadn't any 'idears'.

Swiftly the years went over,
Liquor and drought prevailed;

Middleton went as a drover
  After his station had failed.

Type of a careless nation,
  Men who are soon played out,
Middleton was: — and his station
  Was bought by the Rouseabout.

Flourishing beard and sandy,
  Tall and solid and stout:
This is the picture of Andy,
  Middleton's Rouseabout.

Now on his own dominions
  Works with his overseers;
Hasn't any opinions,
  Hasn't any idears.

HENRY LAWSON

*rouseabout* any unskilled worker on a station or in a shearing shed

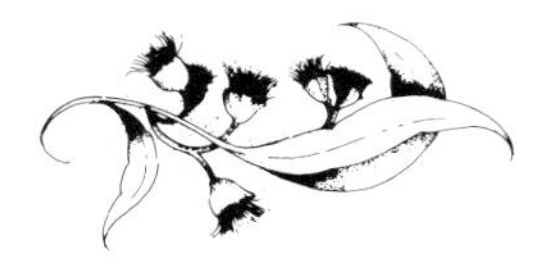

# Freedom on the Wallaby

Our fathers toiled for bitter bread
  While idlers thrived beside them;
But food to eat and clothes to wear
  Their native land denied them.
They left their native land in spite
  Of royalties' regalia,
And so they came, or if they stole
  Were sent out to Australia.

They struggled hard to make a home,
  Hard grubbing 'twas and clearing.
They weren't troubled much with toffs
  When they were pioneering;
And now that we have made the land
  A garden full of promise,
Old greed must crook his dirty hand
  And come to take it from us.

But Freedom's on the Wallaby.
  She'll knock the tyrants silly,
She's going to light another fire
  And boil another billy.
We'll make the tyrants feel the sting
  Of those that they would throttle;
They needn't say the fault is ours
  If blood should stain the wattle.

HENRY LAWSON

# Cockies of Bungaree

Come all you jolly travellers that's out of work, just mind
Take a trip to Bungaree and plenty there you'll find.
Have a trial with the cockies and just take it from me
I'm certain sure you'll rue the day you first saw Bungaree.

And how I came this weary way I mean to let you know
Being out of employment I didn't know where to go.
I called at a registry office and there I did agree
To take a job of clearing for a cocky in Bungaree.

Well on the Monday morning to work I had to go,
My Noble shouted at me, 'Getting up you're rather slow;
Take this pick and shovel, set to work and grub that tree.'
'Oh begob,' says I, ''tis nice and light, this work in Bungaree.'

Well on the Tuesday morning it was the usual go
He called me up to breakfast before the cocks did crow;
The stars were shining gloriously, and the moon was high,
you see,
And I thought before the sun would rise I'd die in Bungaree.

When I went in to supper it was after half past nine
And when I had it ate sure I thought it was bed-time
But the cocky came to me saying with a merry laugh,
'I want you for an hour or two to cut a bit of chaff.'

And while we are chaff-cutting, he says, 'It's quite a spell.'
'Oh begob,' says I, 'it is, and it's I that knows it well.'
We always were a-quarrelling, we never could agree
So at last I made up my mind to leave old Bungaree.

So now my job is over and I'm at liberty
And it's of the cocky's health and wealth I'm spending merrily;
I am not a boasting fellow, no lies I ever told,
So if you will believe me now, it's the truth I did unfold.

ANON.

*cockies* 'cockatoo' farmers, so called by the squatters because they seemed to descend on their runs as destructively as a flock of cockatoos. They continued to be distinguished from the graziers because they had to scratch the earth for a living, and they became a byword for parsimony in the outback.

# Wallaby Stew

Poor Dad, he got five years or more, as everybody knows,
And now he lives in Maitland gaol, broad arrows on
his clothes;
He branded old Brown's cleanskins and he never left a tail
So I'll relate the family's fate since Dad got put in gaol.

*Chorus:*
So stir the wallaby stew, make soup of the kangaroo tail;
I tell you things is pretty tough since Dad got put in gaol.

Our sheep all died a month ago, of footrot and the fluke;
Our cow got shot last Christmas Day by my big brother Luke;
Our mother's got a shearer cove forever within hail;
The family will have grown a bit when Dad gets out of gaol.

Our Bess got shook upon some bloke, but he's gone, we don't
know where;
He used to act about the sheds, but he ain't acted square;
I sold the buggy on my own, and the place is up for sale;
That won't be all that has been junked when Dad comes
out of gaol.

They let Dad out before his time to give us a surprise.
He came and slowly looked around, then gently blessed
our eyes;
He shook hands with the shearer cove, and said that things
seemed stale,
And left him here to shepherd us, and battled back into gaol.

ANON.

*cleanskins* unbranded calves, which could be stolen by anyone fixing his brand on them.

# Nine Miles from Gundagai

I've done my share of shearing sheep,
Of droving, and all that,
And bogged a bullock team as well
On a Murrumbidgee flat.
I've seen the bullock stretch and strain,
And blink his bleary eye,
And the dog sit on the tucker box
Nine miles from Gundagai.

I've been jilted, jarred, and crossed in love,
  And sand-bagged in the dark,
And if a mountain fell on me,
  I'd treat it as a lark.
It's when you've got your bullocks bogged,
  That's the time you flog and cry,
And the dog sits on the tucker box,
  Nine miles from Gundagai.

We've all got our little troubles
  In life's hard, thorny way;
Some strike them in a motor car,
  And others in a dray.
But when your dog and bullocks strike,
  It ain't no apple pie,
And the dog sits on the tucker box,
  Nine miles from Gundagai.

But that's all past and dead and gone,
  And I've sold the team for meat,
And perhaps some day where I was bogged
  There'll be an asphalt street.
The dog — ah! well, he got a bait,
  And thought he'd like to die,
So I buried him — in the tucker box,
  Nine miles from Gundagai.

JACK MOSES

# Shearing in the Bar

My shearing days are over, though I never was a gun:
I could always count my twenty at the end of every run.
I used the old Trade Union shears, and the blades were
running full
As I shoved them to the knockers and I pushed away the wool.
I shore at Goorianawa and never got the sack;
From Breeza out to Comprador I always could go back;
But though I am a truthful man I find, when in a bar,
That my tally's always doubled but — I never call for tar!

Now shearing on the Western Plains, where the fleece is
full of sand
And clover-burr and cork-screw grass, is the place to
try your hand;
For the sheep are tough and wiry where they feed on the
Mitchell Grass,
And every second one of them is close to the 'cobbler' class;
And a pen chocked full of 'cobblers' is a shearer's dream of hell,
And loud and lurid are their words when they catch one
on the bell:
But when we're pouring down the grog you'll hear no call
for tar,
For the shearer never cuts them — when he's shearing
in a bar!

At Louth I got the bell-sheep, a wrinkly tough-woolled brute,
Who never stopped his kicking till I tossed him down the chute.
Though my wrist was aching badly, I fought him all the way:
I couldn't afford to miss a blow — I must earn my pound a day;

So when I took a strip of skin, I would hide it with my knee —
Gently turn the sheep around so the right bower couldn't see,
Then try to catch the rousy's eye, and softly whisper, 'Tar';
But it never seems to happen — when I'm shearing in a bar!

I shore away the belly-wool, and trimmed the crutch and hocks,
Then opened up along the neck, while the rousy swept
the locks,
Then smartly swung the sheep around, and dumped him on his
rear —
Two blows to chip away the wig — (I also took an ear!)
Then down around the shoulder and the blades were
opened wide,
As I drove them on the long blow and down the whipping side;
And when I tossed him down the chute he was nearly black
with tar,
But it never seems to happen — when I'm shearing at the bar!

Now when the season's ended and my grandsons all come back
In their Vanguards and their Holdens — I was always 'on
the track'—
They come and take me into town to fill me up with beer,
And I sit on a corner-stool and listen to them shear:
There's not a bit of difference! It must make the angels weep,
To hear a mob of shearers in a bar-room shearing sheep;
The sheep go rattling down the race and there's never a call
for tar,
For they still don't seem to cut them — when they're shearing
in a bar!

Then memories come crowding and they roll away the years,
And my hands begin to tighten and they seem to feel
the shears:
I want to tell them of the sheds, of sheds where I have shorn,

Full fifty years, or maybe more, before the boys were born.
I want to speak of Yarragreen, Dunlop or Wingadee,
But the beer has started working and I find I cannot see.
So I'd better not start shearing — I'd be bound to call for tar;
Then be treated like a blackleg — when I'm shearing in a bar!

H. P. 'DUKE' TRITTON

*gun* champion
*knockers* pads at the heel of the blades to prevent them from clashing
*cobbler* the sheep left to the last in the pen, as the roughest to shear
*bell-sheep* a sheep taken from the pen just as the bell rings to signal the end of a shift (important to a shearer trying to increase his tally)
*blow* a stroke of the shears
*rousy* the rouseabout, who does the unskilled work in the shed
*whipping side* the last side of the sheep to be shorn

# The Song of the Wattle

The bush was grey a week to-day,
Olive-green and brown and grey,
But now the Spring has come this way
With blossoms for the Wattle.

It seems to be a fairy tree,
It dances to a melody,
And sings a little song to me,
The graceful swaying Wattle.

See how it weaves its feath'ry sheaves!
Before the wind a maze it weaves —

A misty whirl of powd'ry leaves,
The dainty curts'ying Wattle.

Its boughs uplift, an elfin gift,
A spray of yellow, downy drift,
Thro' which the sunbeams shower and sift
Their gold-dust o'er the Wattle.

The bush was grey a week to–day,
Olive-green and brown and grey,
But now it's sunny all the way,
For Oh! the Spring has come to stay
With blossoms for the Wattle.

VERONICA MASON

These verses were recited or sung in New South Wales schools on Wattle Day, 1 August. The music, with the annotation 'cheerfully, but not too fast', is given on the back page of the *School Magazine* for 1 August, 1929.

# Said Hanrahan

'We'll all be rooned,' said Hanrahan
In accents most forlorn
Outside the church ere Mass began
One frosty Sunday morn.

The congregation stood about,
Coat-collars to the ears,

And talked of stock and crops and drought
As it had done for years.

'It's lookin' crook,' said Daniel Croke;
'Bedad, it's cruke, me lad,
For never since the banks went broke
Has seasons been so bad.'

'It's dry, all right,' said young O'Neil,
With which astute remark
He squatted down upon his heel
And chewed a piece of bark.

And so around the chorus ran
'It's keepin' dry, no doubt.'
'We'll all be rooned,' said Hanrahan,
'Before the year is out.

'The crops are done; ye'll have your work
To save one bag of grain;
From here way out to Back-o'-Bourke
They're singin' out for rain.

'They're singin' out for rain,' he said,
'And all the tanks are dry.'
The congregation scratched its head,
And gazed around the sky.

'There won't be grass, in any case,
Enough to feed an ass;
There's not a blade on Casey's place
As I came down to Mass.'

'If rain don't come this month,' said Dan,
And cleared his throat to speak —
'We'll all be rooned,' said Hanrahan,
'If rain don't come this week.'

A heavy silence seemed to steal
On all at this remark;
And each man squatted on his heel,
And chewed a piece of bark.

'We want an inch of rain, we do,'
O'Neil observed at last;
But Croke 'maintained' we wanted two
To put the danger past.

'If we don't get three inches, man,
Or four to break this drought,
We'll all be rooned,' said Hanrahan,
'Before the year is out.'

In God's good time down came the rain;
And all the afternoon
On iron roof and window-pane
It drummed a homely tune.

And through the night it pattered still,
And lightsome, gladsome elves
On dripping spout and window-sill
Kept talking to themselves.

It pelted, pelted all day long,
A-singing at its work,
Till every heart took up the song
Way out to Back-o'-Bourke.

And every creek a banker ran,
And dams filled overtop;
'We'll all be rooned,' said Hanrahan,
'If this rain doesn't stop.'

And stop it did, in God's good time:
And spring came in to fold
A mantle o'er the hills sublime
Of green and pink and gold.

And days went by on dancing feet,
With harvest-hopes immense,
And laughing eyes beheld the wheat
Nid-nodding o'er the fence.

And, oh, the smiles on every face,
As happy lad and lass
Through grass knee-deep on Casey's place
Went riding down to Mass.

While round the church in clothes genteel
Discoursed the men of mark,
And each man squatted on his heel,
And chewed his piece of bark.

'There'll be bush-fires for sure, me man,
There will, without a doubt;
We'll all be rooned,' said Hanrahan,
'Before the year is out.'

P. J. HARTIGAN ('JOHN O'BRIEN')

# Tangmalangaloo

The bishop sat in lordly state and purple cap sublime,
And galvanised the old bush church at Confirmation time;
And all the kids were mustered up from fifty miles around,
With Sunday clothes, and staring eyes, and ignorance profound.
Now was it fate, or was it grace, whereby they yarded too
An overgrown two-storey lad from Tangmalangaloo?

A hefty son of virgin soil, where nature has her fling,
And grows the trefoil three feet high and mats it in the spring;
Where mighty hills unlift their heads to pierce the welkin's rim,
And trees sprout up a hundred feet before they shoot a limb;
There everything is big and grand, and men are giants too —
But Christian Knowledge wilts, alas, at Tangmalangaloo.

The bishop summed the youngsters up, as bishops only can;
He cast a searching glance around, then fixed upon his man.
But glum and dumb and undismayed through every bout he sat;
He seemed to think that he was there, but wasn't sure of that.
The bishop gave a scornful look, as bishops sometimes do,
And glared right through the pagan in from Tangmalangaloo.

'Come, tell me, boy,' his lordship said in crushing tones severe,
'Come, tell me why is Christmas Day the greatest of the year?
How is it that around the world we celebrate that day
And send a name upon a card to those who're far away?
Why is it wandering ones return with smiles and
greetings, too?'
A squall of knowledge hit the lad from Tangmalangaloo.

He gave a lurch which set a-shake the vases on the shelf,
He knocked the benches all askew, up-ending of himself.
And oh, how pleased his lordship was, and how he smiled to say,
'That's good, my boy. Come, tell me now; and what is
Christmas Day?'
The ready answer bared a fact no bishop ever knew —
'It's the day before the races out at Tangmalangaloo.'

P. J. HARTIGAN ('JOHN O'BRIEN')

# Fourteen Men

Fourteen men,
And each hung down,
Straight as a log
From his toes to his crown.

Fourteen men —
Chinamen they were,
Hanging on the trees
By their pigtailed hair.

Honest poor men,
But the diggers said, Nay!
So they strung them all up,
On a fine summer's day.

There they were hanging
As we came by,
Grown-ups on the front seat,
On the back seat I.

That was Lambing Flat,
And still I can see
The straight up and down
Of each on his tree.

MARY GILMORE

*Lambing Flat* The anti-Chinese riots on the goldfields at Lambing Flat (the present-day Young) occurred in 1861, before Mary Gilmore was born. The Chinese were brutally attacked, but there was no loss of life.

# Country Towns

Country towns, with your willows and squares,
And farmers bouncing on barrel mares
To public-houses of yellow wood
With '1860' over their doors,
And that mysterious race of Hogans
Which always keeps General Stores . . .

At the School of Arts, a broadsheet lies
Sprayed with the sarcasm of flies:
'The Great Golightly Family

Of Entertainers Here To-night' —
Dated a year and a half ago,
But left there, less from carelessness
Than from a wish to seem polite.

Verandas baked with musky sleep,
Mulberry faces dozing deep,
And dogs that lick the sunlight up
Like paste of gold — or, roused in vain
By far, mysterious buggy-wheels,
Lower their ears, and drowse again . . .

Country towns with your schooner bees,
And locusts burnt in the pepper-trees,
Drown me with syrups, arch your boughs,
Find me a bench, and let me snore,
Till, charged with ale and unconcern,
I'll think it's noon at half-past four!

KENNETH SLESSOR

# Crow Country

Gutted of station, noise alone,
The crow's voice trembles down the sky
As if this nitrous flange of stone
Wept suddenly with such a cry;

As if the rock found lips to sigh,
The riven earth a mouth to moan;
But we that hear them, stumbling by,
Confuse their torments with our own.

Over the huge abraded rind,
Crow-countries graped with dung, we go,
Past gullies that no longer flow
And wells that nobody can find,
Lashed by the screaming of the crow,
Stabbed by the needles of the mind.

KENNETH SLESSOR

# *Remittance Man*

The spendthrift, disinherited and graceless,
accepted his pittance with an easy air,
only surprised he could escape so simply
from the pheasant-shooting and the aunts in the
close;
took to the life, dropped easily out of knowledge,
and tramping the backtracks in the summer haze
let everything but life slip through his fingers.

Blue blowing smoke of twigs from the noon fire,
red blowing dust of roads where the teams go slow,
sparse swinging shadow of trees no longer foreign
silted the memory of a greener climate.

The crazy tales, the hatters' crazy secrets,
the blind-drunk sprees indifferently forgiven,
and past them all, the track to escape and nowhere
suited his book, the freak who could never settle.
That pale stalk of a wench at the country ball
sank back forgotten in black Mary's eyes,
and past the sallow circle of the plains' horizon
faded the rainy elms seen through the nursery
window.

That harsh biblical country of the scapegoat
closed its magnificence finally round his bones
polished by diligent ants. The squire his brother,
presuming death, sighed over the documents,
and lifting his eyes across the inherited garden
let a vague pity blur the formal roses.

JUDITH WRIGHT

# South of my Days

South of my days' circle, part of my blood's country,
rises that tableland, high delicate outline
of bony slopes wincing under the winter;
low trees blue-leaved and olive; outcropping granite —
clean, lean, hungry country. The creek's leaf-silenced,
willow-choked, the slope a tangle of medlar and crab-apple,
branching over and under, blotched with a green lichen;
and the old cottage lurches in for shelter.

O cold the black-frost night. The walls draw in to the warmth
and the old roof cracks its joints; the slung kettle
hisses a leak on the fire. Hardly to be believed that summer
will turn up again some day in a wave of rambler roses,
thrust its hot face in here to tell another yarn —
a story old Dan can spin into a blanket against the winter.
Seventy years of stories he clutches round his bones.
Seventy summers are hived in him like old honey.

Droving that year, Charleville to the Hunter,
nineteen-one it was, and the drought beginning;
sixty head left at the McIntyre, the mud round them
hardened like iron; and the yellow boy died
in the sulky ahead with the gear, but the horse went on,
stopped at the Sandy Camp and waited in the evening.
It was the flies we seen first, swarming like bees.
Came to the Hunter, three hundred head of a thousand —
cruel to keep them alive — and the river was dust.

Or mustering up in the Bogongs in the autumn
when the blizzards came early. Brought them down; we
brought them
down, what aren't there yet. Or driving for Cobb's on the run
up from Tamworth — Thunderbolt at the top of Hungry Hill,
and I give him a wink. I wouldn't wait long, Fred,
not if I was you; the troopers are just behind,
coming for that job at the Hillgrove. He went like a luny,
him on his big black horse.

Oh, they slide and they vanish
as he shuffles the years like a pack of conjuror's cards.
True or not, it's all the same; and the frost on the roof
cracks like a whip, and the back-log breaks into ash.
Wake, old man. This is winter, and the yarns are over.
No one is listening.

South of my days' circle
I know it dark against the stars, the high lean country
full of old stories that still go walking in my sleep.

JUDITH WRIGHT

## Up-country Pubs

Each four-square limestone monument
Of praise to man's heroic thirsts
Heaves elementally and bursts
With gusty, shirt-sleeved merriment.

And though verandas loll and sprawl
Or windows arch their lidless eyes,
And leaning posts apostrophise
The unsafe step and sagging wall,

Yet Spring in street and paddock hurls
Its sap till every corner brims,
And morning jumps along the limbs
Of singing trees and ready girls.

With breasts and buttocks firm as trees
The barmaid-waitress blooms and sways,
And drinking timber-men appraise
How thighs grow upwards from the knees;

All day they dream and climb astride
Such satin-smooth and supple forks,
And cling and linger in their talks
Of stems so straight and scarfs so wide;

And tractor-drivers' glances state
That doors they know of have no locks
And love wears deftly-zippered frocks
When sudden Spring and moonlight mate.

And shearers ask for leg and tart:
No matter what the table lacks
These come to them as midnight snacks,
Kept hot and served with lusty art.

And in the Bar and Men's redoubt
Gargantuan drinkers handle beer

With massive feet apart, and steer
It grandly in or grandly out.

Australia Fair pursues its way,
And in its myth of malt and mirth
The nation's salt still goes to earth
On each up-country Saturday.

COLIN THIELE

# Sydney and the Bush

When Sydney and the Bush first met
there was no open ground
and men and girls, in chains and not,
all made an urgent sound.

Then convicts bled and warders bred,
the Bush went back and back,
the men of Fire and of Earth
became White men and Black.

When Sydney ordered lavish books
and warmed her feet with coal
the Bush came skylarking to town
and gave poor folk a soul.

Then bushmen sank and factories rose
and warders set the tone —
the Bush, in quarter-acre blocks,
helped families hold their own.

When Sydney and the Bush meet now
there is antipathy
and fashionable suburbs float
at night, far out to sea.

When Sydney rules without the Bush
she is a warders' shop
with heavy dancing overhead
the music will not stop

and when the drummers want a laugh
Australians are sent up.
When Sydney and the Bush meet now
there is no common ground.

LES A. MURRAY

# Index of Titles

# Index of First Lines

# Acknowledgements

'Country Towns', 'Crow Country', Kenneth Slessor; copyright Paul Slessor, 1944

'Fourteen Men', Mary Gilmore; copyright the Estate of Dame Mary Gilmore, 1954

'My Country', Dorothea Mackellar; reproduced by permission of the Estate of Dorothea Mackellar, c/o Curtis Brown (Aust) Pty Ltd

'Said Hanrahan', 'Tangmalangaloo', P. J. Hartigan (J. P. O'Brien); copyright F. A. Mecham, 1921

'South of my Days', 'Remittance Man', Judith Wright; reproduced by permission of Judith Wright

'Sydney and the Bush', Les A. Murray; reproduced by permission of Les A. Murray

'Up-country Pubs', Colin Thiele; Colin Thiele

*Every effort has been made to contact and acknowledge copyright holders. The publishers would be pleased to hear from any copyright holders they were unable to contact.*